Date: 2/21/18

J 796.334 MIL
Stewart, Mark,
A.C. Milan /

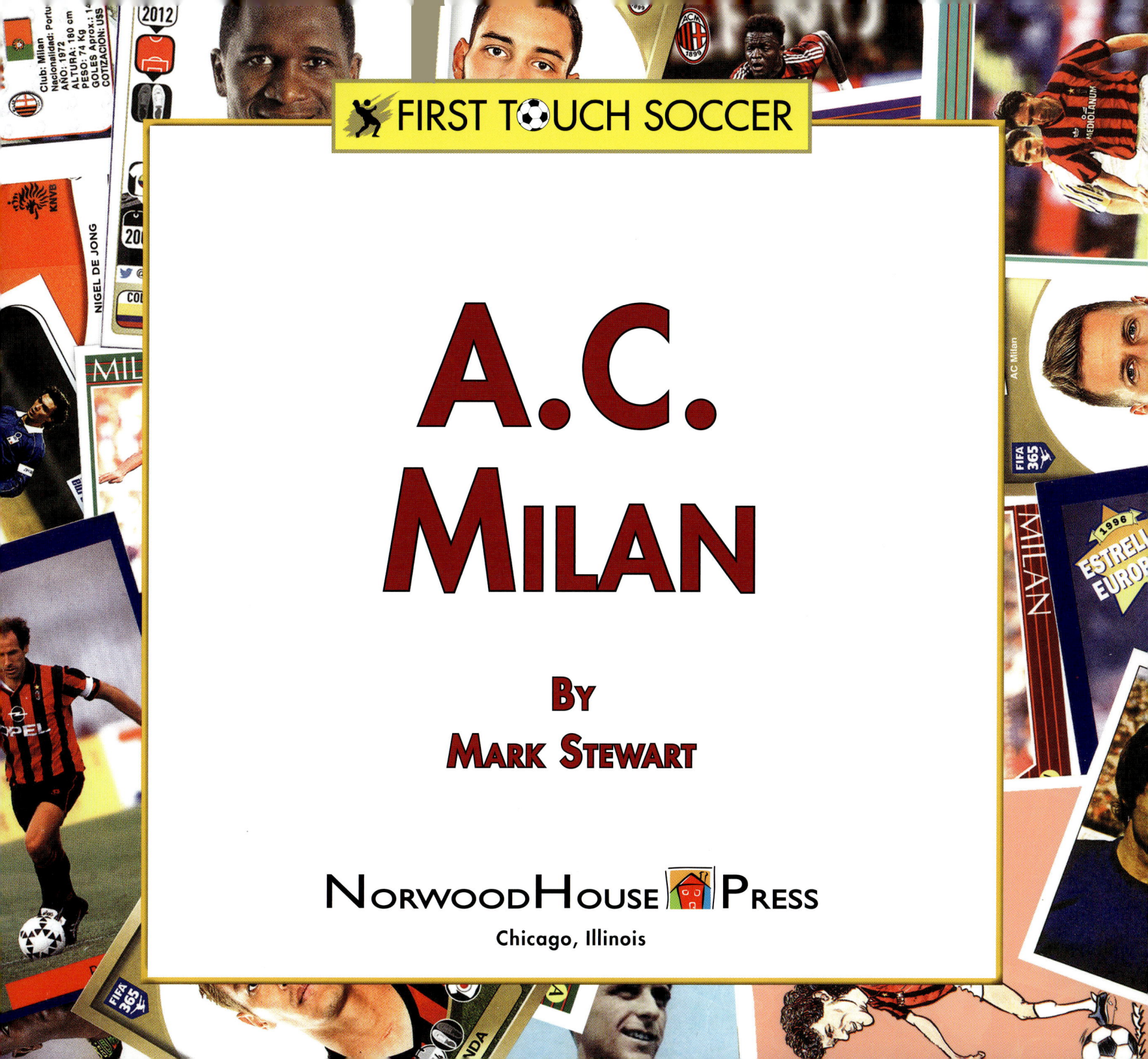

FIRST TOUCH SOCCER

A.C. Milan

By Mark Stewart

Norwood House Press
Chicago, Illinois

P.O. Box 316598 • Chicago, Illinois 60631
For more information about Norwood House Press please visit our website at www.norwoodhousepress.com or call 866-565-2900.

Photography and Collectibles:
The trading cards and other memorabilia assembled in the background for this book's cover and interior pages are all part of the author's collection and are reproduced for educational and artistic purposes.

All photos courtesy of Associated Press except the following individual photos and artifacts (page numbers):
Author's Collection (6, 10 both), Score (11 top & middle, 22), World Soccer/IPC Media (11 bottom), Juego del 5 (16).

Cover image: Matteo Bazzi/Associated Press

Designer: Ron Jaffe
Series Editor: Mike Kennedy
Content Consultants: Michael Jacobsen and Jonathan Wentworth-Ping
Project Management: Black Book Partners, LLC
Editorial Production: Lisa Walsh

LIBRARY OF CONGRESS CATALOGING-IN-PUBLICATION DATA
Names: Stewart, Mark, 1960 July 7- author.
Title: A.C. Milan / By Mark Stewart.
Description: Chicago Illinois : Norwood House Press, 2017. | Series: First
  Touch Soccer | Includes bibliographical references and index. | Audience:
  Age 5-8. | Audience: K to Grade 3.
Identifiers: LCCN 2016058208 (print) | LCCN 2017005796 (ebook) | ISBN
  9781599538556 (library edition : alk. paper) | ISBN 9781684040742 (eBook)
Subjects: LCSH: Milan (Soccer team)--History--Juvenile literature.
Classification: LCC GV943.6.M54 S84 2017 (print) | LCC GV943.6.M54 (ebook) |
  DDC 796.334/640945211--dc23
LC record available at https://lccn.loc.gov/2016058208

©2018 by Norwood House Press. All rights reserved.
No part of this book may be reproduced without written permission from the publisher.

This publication is intended for educational purposes and is not affiliated with any team, league, or association including: Associazione Calcio Milan S.p.A., Lega Nazionale Professionalisti Serie A, The Union of European Football Associations (UEFA), or the Federation Internationale de Football Association (FIFA).

302N--072017
Manufactured in the United States of America in North Mankato, Minnesota.

Contents

Meet A.C. Milan 5
Time Machine 6
Best Seat in the House 9
Collector's Corner 10
Worthy Opponents 12
Club Ways 14
On the Map 16
Kit and Crest 19
We Won! 20
For the Record 22
Soccer Words 24
Index 24
About the Author 24

Words in **bold type** are defined on page 24.

In soccer, star players often go by a one-word nickname. In this book, we use the nickname followed by the player's (*full name*).

Yeah! Juraj Kucka celebrates a goal during a Serie A match against Chievo in 2016. Serie A is Italy's top-level soccer league.

Meet A.C. Milan

The city of Milan is one of the largest in Europe. More than 5 million people live in or near Milan. Soccer has been their favorite sport for more than 100 years. The city's oldest team is called Associazione Calcio Milan, or A.C. Milan for short. Calcio is the Italian word for soccer.

Another club, Internazionale Milan, also plays in the city. To keep from confusing the two, soccer fans call A.C. Milan "Milan" and Internazionale Milan "Inter."

Time Machine

In 1899, two Englishmen living in Milan formed a club to play soccer and cricket. Two years later, the soccer team won its first Italian title. During the 1950s, Milan became one of the best clubs in Europe.

The club won major championships in the 1960s, 1970s, 1980s, 1990s, and 2000s. Its great stars include Gunnar Nordhal, **Juan Alberto Schiaffino**, Gianni Rivera, and Paolo Maldini.

Paolo Maldini beats an opponent to the ball with help from teammate Gianluca Zambrotta.

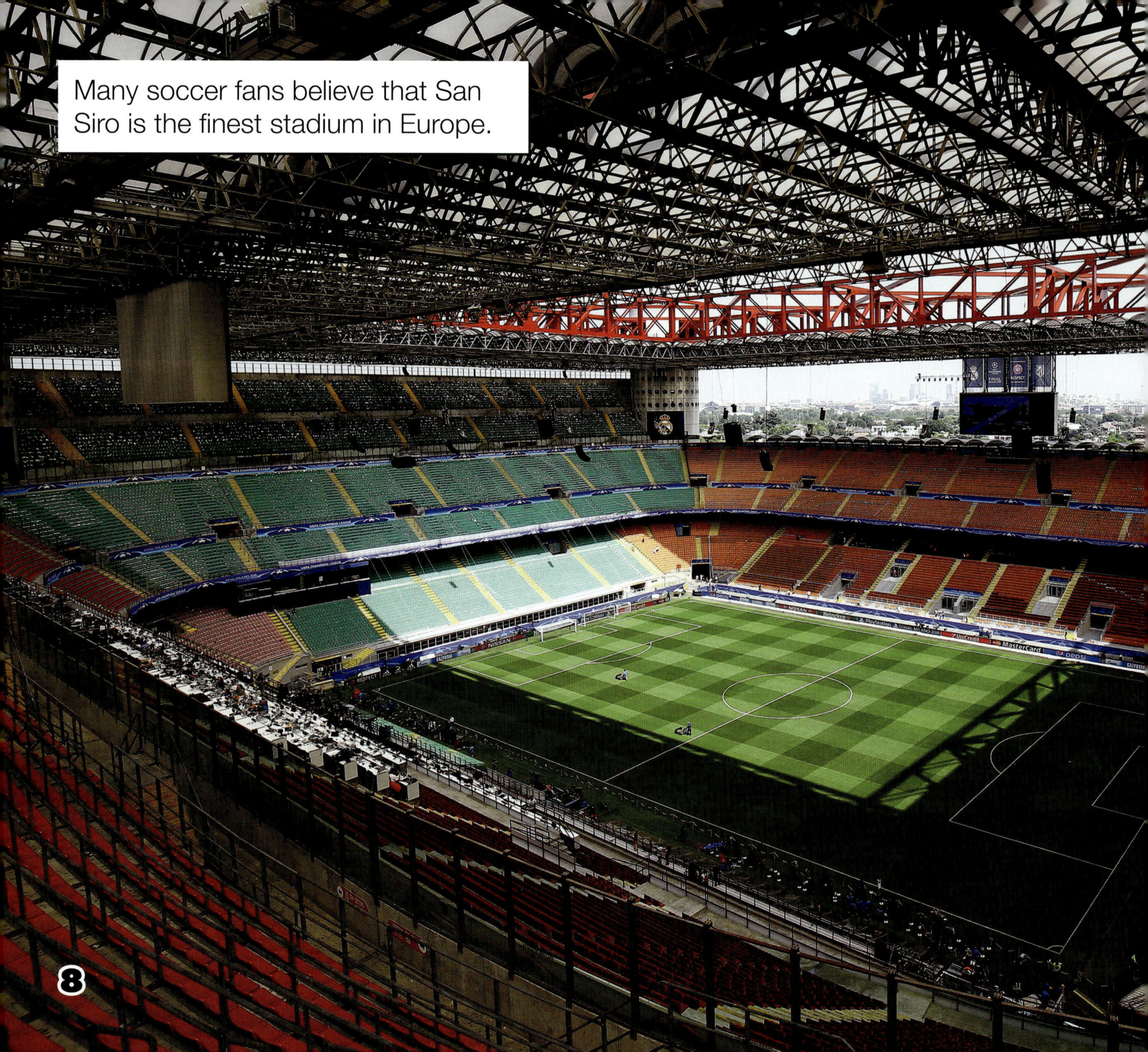
Many soccer fans believe that San Siro is the finest stadium in Europe.

Best Seat in the House

A.C. Milan plays its home **matches** in Giuseppe Meazza Stadium. Meazza was an Italian star of the 1930s and 1940s. The fans call the stadium San Siro, after the part of the city where it is located. Milan shares San Siro with its greatest rival, Inter Milan. The stadium holds more than 80,000 people.

Collector's Corner

These collectibles show some of the best Milan players ever.

Gunnar Gren
Midfielder/Forward
1949–1953
Gren was one of three stars from Sweden on the team. Gren, Gunnar Nordhal, and Nils Liedholm were called "Gre-No-Li" by Milan fans.

Gianni Rivera
Midfielder
1960–1979
Rivera was a skilled and clever player. He was always finding new ways to lead Milan's attack.

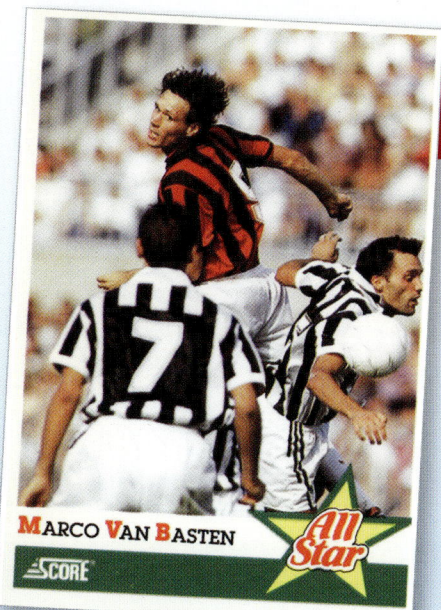

MARCO VAN BASTEN

Forward
1987–1995

Milan fans had never seen a scorer like van Basten. He was named the top player in Europe three times between 1988 and 1992.

ROBERTO DONADONI

Midfielder
1986–1996 & 1997–1999

Donadoni never got tired and rarely made a mistake. He had the talent to play any position on the field.

PAOLO MALDINI

Defender
1985–2009

Maldini played his first match for Milan at 16. He became one of the best defensive players in the history of the sport.

Worthy Opponents

Milan shares the same field with Inter Milan, its top rival since 1908. Back then, Milan fans were mostly factory workers. They were nicknamed Casciavit, which is Italian for "Screwdrivers." Inter Milan fans were wealthier people. They were nicknamed Bauscia, which means "Big Shots" or "Show-offs." Now both teams have millions of fans from every walk of life.

Philippe Mexes heads the ball toward a teammate in a match against Inter Milan.

Club Ways

Milan soccer fans can be very superstitious. So can the players. The most famous was Filippo Inghazi. He could not begin a game without opening a box of cookies. Inghazi would eat until there were only two cookies left. Then he was ready for action. The cookies really worked in 2002–03. That season, he scored 30 goals for Milan!

What looks like the entire city has turned out to cheer for the players after their 18th Serie A title, in 2011. Superstitious Milan fans would not dare miss a victory parade!

On the Map

Milan brings together players from many countries. These are some of the best:

1. **Nils Liedholm** • Valdemarsvik, Sweden
2. **Frank Rijkaard** • Amsterdam, Netherlands
3. **Rui Costa** • Amadora, Portugal
4. **Andriy Shevchenko** • Dvirkivshchyna, Ukraine
5. **George Weah** • Monrovia, Liberia
6. **Clarence Seedorf** • Paramaribo, Suriname
7. **Kaka (*Ricardo Izecson dos Santos Leite*)** • Gama, Brazil
8. **Juan Alberto Schiaffino** • Montevideo, Uruguay

Map of Europe

A.C. Milan's home stadium is in Milan, Italy.

World Map

Milan's red-and-black club crest can be seen under the white star on Mattia De Sciglio's uniform.

Kit and Crest

Milan's club colors have not changed since 1899. Red was picked to show the fire of the players. Black was picked to show the fear teams had when they played Milan. The players wear red and black shirts for home matches. The team's away **kit** is mostly white. The club's crest shows the club's colors and the flag of Milan. The letters ACM stand for Associazione Calcio Milan.

We Won!

The 1988–89 season is one Milan fans will never forget. Marco van Basten, Ruud Gullit, and Frank Rijkaard each scored in a 5–0 win against powerful Real Madrid in the **European Cup**. That victory set up a championship match against the number-one team in Romania. Gullit and van Basten scored twice each to win, 4–0. It was Milan's first European Cup in 20 years. The club won the tournament again in 1990!

Frank Rijkaard shows off the European Cup after Milan's 1990 victory. He was one of three Dutch stars on the club, along with Marco van Basten and Ruud Gullit.

For the Record

These Milan players have been named European Footballer of the Year:

1969   Gianni Rivera

1987   **Ruud Gullit**

1988   Marco van Basten

1989   Marco van Basten

1992   Marco van Basten

1995   George Weah

2004   Andriy Shevchenko

2007   Kaka

Milan has won more than 60 major championships!

Italian Football League/Serie A

18 championships (from 1901 to 2011)

Coppa Italia*

1966–67
1971–72
1972–73
1976–77
2002–03

Cup Winners' Cup

1967–68
1972–73

World Club Cup

2007

European Cup/Champions League

1962–63
1968–69
1988–89
1989–90
1993–94
2002–03
2006–07

Super Cup

1989
1990
1994
2003
2007

*The Coppa Italia (Italy Cup) is a competition among all the pro teams in Italy.

Soccer Words

European Cup
A competition among the top clubs in Europe. Today the tournament is called the Champions League.

Kit
The official league equipment of soccer players, including a club's uniform.

Matches
Another word for games. Soccer matches are 90 minutes long. Each half is 45 minutes, with a 15-minute break in between.

Index

Costa, Rui	16
De Sciglio, Mattia	**18**
Donadoni, Roberto	11, **11**
Gren, Gunnar	10, **10**
Gullit, Ruud	20, **21**, 22, **22**
Inghazi, Filippo	14
Kaka	16, 22
Kucka, Juraj	**4**
Liedholm, Nils	10, 16
Maldini, Paolo	6, **7**, 11, **11**
Meazza, Giuseppe	9
Mexes, Philippe	**13**
Nordhal, Gunnar	6, 10
Rijkaard, Frank	16, 20, **21**
Rivera, Gianni	6, 10, **10**, 22
Schiaffino, Juan Alberto	6, **6**, 16
Seedorf, Clarence	16
Shevchenko, Andriy	16, **16**, 22
van Basten, Marco	11, **11**, 20, **21**, 22
Weah, George	16, 22
Zambrotta, Gianluca	**7**

Photos are on **BOLD** numbered pages.

About the Author

Mark Stewart has been writing about world soccer since the 1990s, including *Soccer: A History of the World's Most Popular Game.* In 2005, he co-authored Major League Soccer's 10-year anniversary book.

About A.C. Milan

Learn more at these websites:
www.acmilan.com/en
www.fifa.com
www.teamspiritextras.com